Lila and Andy learn about

The Journey of Water!

From the River to the Tap

Revised & Updated Second Edition

Kenneth Adams

Book Cover by Kenneth Adams
Illustrations and Images by Kenneth Adams
Illustrations and Images created with AI Assistance
Second Edition 2025

ISBN: 978-1-998552-29-0

To the engineers of tomorrow. Make good choices.

This book belongs to:

_____

Hi, I'm Lila. My world is filled with words. Not just the kind you speak, but the kind that comes alive on paper, in books, just waiting to be discovered.

I take storytelling very seriously. I'm nearly always glued to a book, either reading or scribbling away, creating my own characters, and sending them on daring missions.

While I love getting lost in a good story, there's also a part of me that's always eager to explore and learn about something new and exciting.

Hi there, my name is Andy, and I'm Lila's brother. While I don't read as much as she does, I'm obsessed with figuring out how stuff works.

My experiments can sometimes backfire, and while I love taking apart gadgets to see how they operate, Mom doesn't always like it when I do that, especially when I forget how to put it back together again.

I'm always eager to learn more about the world around us, and I just love doing that with Lila. Like glue, we always stick together.

Andy and I want to share with you what we learned from our dad, a Civil Engineer, about the amazing process of how drinking water is cleaned and delivered to us.

Sometimes we get so used to the convenience of just opening a tap when we are thirsty that we forget how fortunate we are, and how much work is involved in bringing that clean, clear water to our homes and businesses.

Water is very important for life on Earth. All living things, no matter how big or small, need water to survive. In nature, water can come from many different places. The place where water comes from is called a water source. <u>Water sources</u> can be grouped into two main types: surface water and groundwater.

<u>Surface water</u> is all the water you can see on Earth's surface. Things like rivers, streams, lakes, ponds, and even the ocean all contain surface water.

<u>Groundwater</u> is the water found underground, beneath the Earth's surface, in the spaces between the soil and rocks. Groundwater can move slowly through underground rock formations called aquifers, almost like an underground river.

Before we can use water, we first have to collect it, and there are a few different ways to do that.

Surface water can be drawn directly from rivers or lakes, or we can build dams to create giant "water tanks" to store the water in. The water is then pulled from these water sources by using special structures called water intake structures. These structures work like giant straws by using pumps to suck the water from the source into pipes.

Groundwater can be collected by drilling holes deep into the ground and then using pumps to suck the water up to the surface through pipes.

A water intake structure uses water pumps to suck water from the source and discharge it into pipes.

Water that comes from rivers, lakes, dams, or from underground usually has dirt, bugs, leaves, and twigs in it. Some of the little creatures in the water may be so small that we can't even see them. Before we can drink the water, we have to clean it. Otherwise, the stuff that's in it may make us very sick.

Water that has not been cleaned yet is called <u>raw water</u>. Once the raw water is collected from the water source, it flows through pipes to a special place where it will be treated to make it clean. This place is called a <u>Water Treatment Plant</u>, or a Water Purification Plant, since the raw water is "purified" or cleaned before we use it.

Water treatment plants come in all shapes and sizes. If you live in a small town, the water treatment plant may look much different from a water treatment plant in a big city. In fact, it is not uncommon for very big cities to have more than one water treatment plant. The size and layout depend on two main things: how much water the treatment plant has to clean, and how dirty the water is when it arrives.

Water from a clean mountain lake needs less cleaning than water from a muddy river, so the treatment plant can be smaller and simpler. Water that has more dirt, algae, or other stuff floating in it needs bigger tanks and more cleaning steps to make it safe to drink.

It is the job of a <u>Civil Engineer</u> to determine how big the water treatment plant has to be, and which cleaning steps are needed to provide enough clean water for everyone in the community, town, or city.

At the water treatment plant, the water takes a special trip through a number of different cleaning processes. Even though water treatment plants may be different from each other in size and layout, the basic steps for cleaning the water are mostly the same everywhere.

Before we dive into the details of how the water is cleaned, you should know that some of the cleaning processes have long and difficult names. We'll try our best to explain each process as best we can.

Are you up for the challenge? Let's do this!!!

The Water Treatment Process

Step 1: Screening

When the raw water enters the water treatment plant, the first cleaning step is to remove large floating objects like leaves, twigs, and other material we don't want in the water.

This is done by making the water flow through or over large metal screens. A screen is a special piece of equipment that traps the leaves and sticks, while the water flows through it.

When Mom cooks spaghetti, she uses a strainer to separate the spaghetti from the water once it is cooked. The strainer allows the water to run through the tiny holes, while the spaghetti stays behind in the strainer. This is how screens work as well. The water passes through the screen, while the unwanted objects stay behind.

The Water Treatment Process

Step 2: Clarification

While many of the large floating objects are removed during screening, the bugs and dirt that are too small to be trapped by the screens are still floating around in the water.

During clarification, these very small pieces of dirt and other stuff are removed to provide clarified water. Clarified water means all the hard, solid objects and particles have been removed to leave only the clean, clear water.

Clarification happens in three stages:

Stage 1 - Coagulation

Stage 2 - Flocculation

Stage 3 - Sedimentation

Coagulation

Imagine it is your birthday, and you invite all your cool friends to a pool party in your swimming pool. Afterwards, there's all sorts of stuff floating around in the pool, tiny leaves, sand and dirt, perhaps even some party streamers and parts of popped balloons.

While you are cleaning the pool, you find it's very difficult to remove each little piece of waste one by one. But what if you could add something to the water that makes all the small pieces stick together to form big chunks? Wouldn't it be easier to remove the bigger pieces?

This is how <u>coagulation</u> works. Special chemicals, usually harmless salts, are added to the water that make all the waste and dirt stick together to form bigger chunks.

How Coagulation Works

Chemicals being added to the raw water

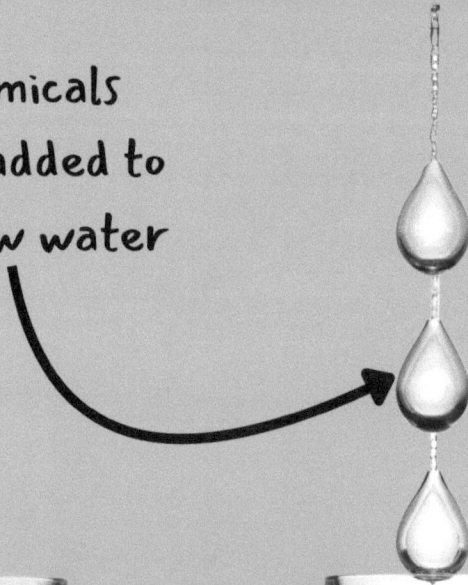

Raw water with dirt particles enter the coagulation tank

+

Chemicals are added to the raw water

=

The chemicals make the dirt particles clump together

Flocculation

During <u>flocculation</u>, the water is mixed with paddles, almost like a giant cake mixer, stirring the water in the flocculation tank slowly, causing the chunks that were formed during coagulation to bump into each other and stick together even more.

The more these chunks bump into each other, the bigger they get and the heavier they become, almost like when you roll a snowball down a snowy hill. These larger, heavier chunks are called <u>flocs.</u> They even look like snowflakes!

Sedimentation

During <u>sedimentation</u>, the water is left to stay really, really still. Because the flocs that formed during coagulation and flocculation are heavier than water, they slowly sink to the bottom of the tank. The longer we wait, the more flocs will settle at the bottom, leaving the cleaner water on top.

The clear water from the top of the tank can then be carefully removed, leaving the dirty settlement, also called sediment, behind!

How Sedimentation Works

During sedimentation, the heavier flocs
settle at the bottom of the tank, leaving
the clean, clear water at the top.

The Water Treatment Process

Step 3: Filtration

Once all the flocs have settled, the clear water removed from the top of the sedimentation tank is passed through <u>filters</u>. Filters act like giant sieves, allowing the clean water to pass through, but making little bits of dirt still left in the water to stay behind.

Think of it this way. When Dad makes a cup of coffee, he first scoops the coffee grounds into a coffee filter, and then he pours hot water through it. What ends up in the cup is just the clean and delicious coffee, while all the coffee grounds stay behind in the filter. A water filter works in a similar way, but instead of coffee grounds, it catches all the tiny bits we don't want in our drinking water!

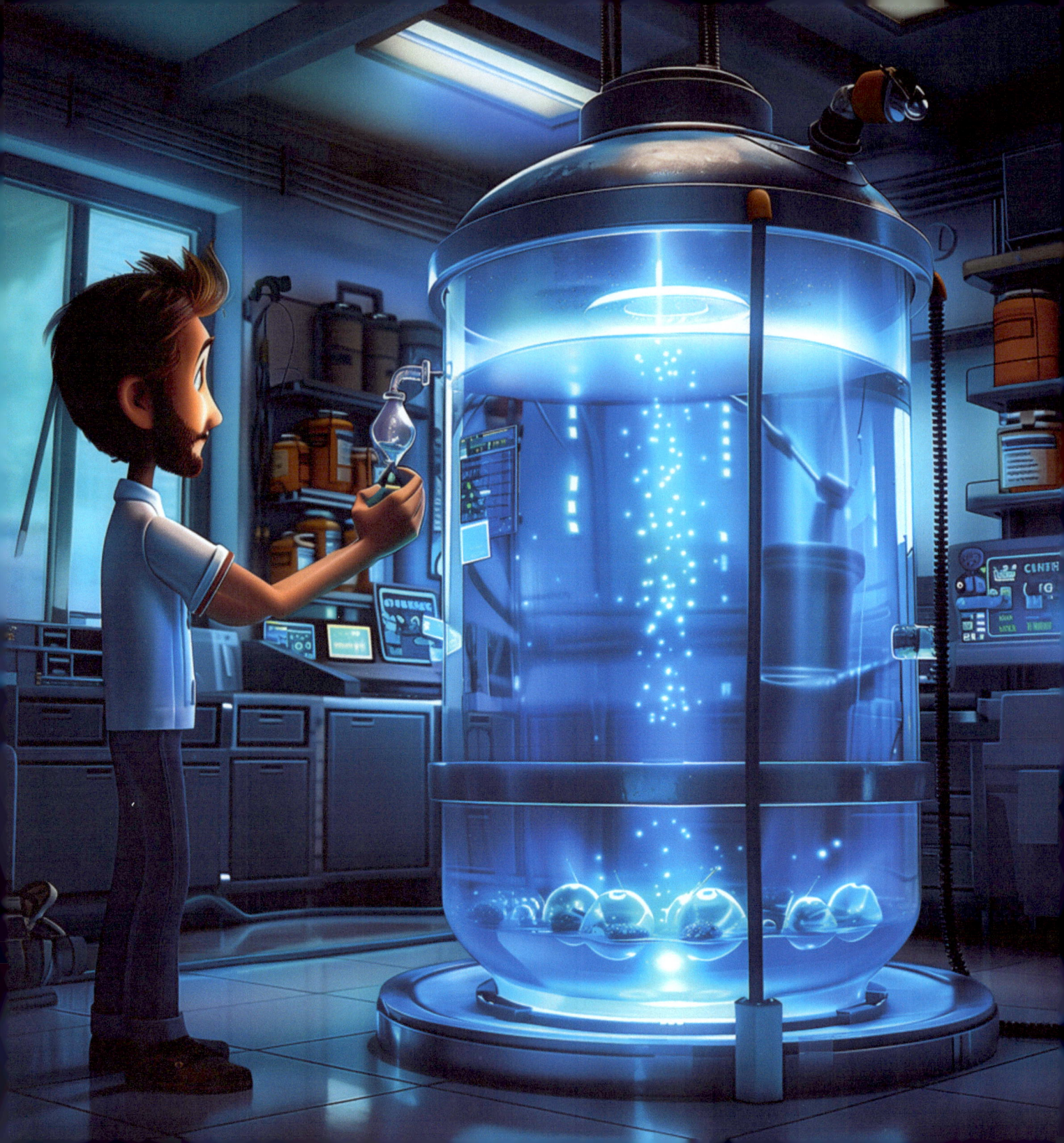

The Water Treatment Process

Step 4: Disinfection

Up to this point of the cleaning process, tiny pieces of dirt clumped together during coagulation and flocculation to form floc. The flocs were then allowed to sink to the bottom of the tank during sedimentation, and the remaining leaves and dirt were removed during filtration.

While the water may look pretty clean by now, there are still some tiny germs swimming around that we can't see. During disinfection, chemicals like chlorine, or sometimes even special ultraviolet light, are added to the water to kill any remaining bacteria or viruses that could make us sick.

The Water Treatment Process

Step 5: Testing

Once all the steps to clean the water have been completed, the water is tested to make sure it's clean enough to drink.

Testing is when a team of engineers and scientists checks the water with special tools to search for any tiny germs that might still be hiding in the water. If the tests show the water is perfectly clean, then it's ready for us to drink.

If, however, the tests show the water is still not clean enough, the water treatment plant will clean the water even more, until it's clean enough to pass the tests.

After all that cleaning at the water treatment plant, the water is ready to go to our homes and schools. To get there, it has to travel through a <u>water distribution system</u>, also called a <u>water supply system</u>, because it "supplies" water to the place where we need it.

A water supply system consists of a number of separate parts that all work together to transport the clean, fresh water to our homes, schools, and places of work.

Let's look at some of the parts that make up a water supply system.

Since we don't want to use up all the clean water that leaves the water treatment plant right away, we can save it up for when we need it the most, like during those hot summer days when everyone might be thirsty.

Water can be safely stored in <u>water storage tanks and reservoirs</u>. These are basically giant containers that store the clean water until we need it at home, at school, or anywhere else we want a refreshing drink!

Storage tanks and reservoirs come in many different forms, from tall water towers to big square or circular tanks. Water storage tanks can be built above or below ground.

A Concrete Reservoir

A Square Steel Tank

A Circular Steel Tank

A Concrete Water Tower

To bring the clean water from the storage tanks and reservoirs all the way to our homes, the water travels through a giant network of underground pipes.

<u>Water pipes</u> look a bit like straws, but they are much sturdier, and can be made of materials like concrete, steel, or plastic.

The clean water travels through these pipes under pressure, kind of like when you squirt water through a squirt gun.

Sometimes the water has to travel quite far to get to all the areas of a town or city, and the water may need some help to flow along the pipes, especially when it has to travel uphill. That's when pump stations are used.

Inside a pump station, pumps are installed to push the water along, forcing it through the pipes with enough pressure to reach even the tallest buildings.

When you open the tap at home, the clean water has traveled all the way from the river to a water treatment plant, into a storage tank or reservoir, and then through a network of pipes all the way to your house!

What an awesome journey!

The next time you see a water treatment plant, a water tower, or a pump station, think of all the work involved to make sure the water we drink at home is clean and safe!

Careers in Raw Water Treatment and Distribution

If you care about providing clean, safe, and reliable water to places where people live, work, and play, then careers dedicated to water treatment and distribution might be perfect for you! There are many exciting jobs for people who want to help create the systems that keep our communities healthy and thriving. Here are examples of careers that work together to bring clean water to every tap.

Engineering & Design:

- <u>Civil Engineer</u> - Designs water treatment plants and distribution systems, deciding how big facilities need to be and where pipes should go.
- <u>Environmental Engineer</u> - Focuses on protecting the environment while cleaning water and making sure the process is safe for nature.
- <u>Water Resources Engineer</u> - Plans how to collect water from rivers, lakes, and underground sources efficiently.
- <u>Chemical Engineer</u> - Designs the chemical processes used in coagulation, flocculation, and disinfection.
- <u>Mechanical Engineer</u> - Designs pumps, motors, and moving equipment that push water through the system.
- <u>Electrical Engineer</u> - Creates the electrical systems that power pumps, lights, and computer controls in treatment plants.
- <u>Process Engineer</u> - Plans the step-by-step cleaning process to make sure water moves efficiently from dirty to clean.
- <u>Systems Engineer</u> - Makes sure all the different parts of the water system work together smoothly.
- <u>Hydraulic Engineer</u> - Specializes in how water flows through pipes and designs systems to control water pressure.

Plant Operations & Maintenance:

- <u>Water Treatment Plant Operator</u> - Runs the daily operations of cleaning water, monitoring each step from screening to disinfection
- <u>Water Distribution System Operator</u> - Controls the flow of clean water through pipes to homes and businesses
- <u>Pump Station Operator</u> - Manages the pumps that push water uphill and maintain proper pressure in the system
- <u>Control Room Operator</u> - Monitors computer screens and controls that track water flow and quality throughout the system
- <u>Maintenance Technician</u> - Fixes and maintains equipment like screens, mixers, and filters to keep everything running
- <u>Instrumentation Technician</u> - Maintains the special tools and sensors that measure water quality and system performance
- <u>Electrician</u> - Repairs and maintains all electrical equipment in treatment plants and pump stations
- <u>Millwright</u> - Installs, moves, and repairs heavy machinery like large pumps and motors
- <u>Pipefitter/Plumber</u> - Installs and repairs the pipes that carry water through the treatment and distribution system

Laboratory & Quality Control:

- <u>Water Quality Technician</u> - Tests water samples to make sure they meet safety standards before reaching homes.
- <u>Laboratory Analyst</u> - Uses special equipment to check for chemicals, bacteria, and other substances in water samples.
- <u>Microbiologist</u> - Studies tiny germs and bacteria in water to ensure disinfection processes are working properly.
- <u>Chemist</u> - Analyzes the chemical makeup of water and determines what chemicals are needed for treatment.
- <u>Environmental Scientist</u> - Studies how water treatment affects the environment and ensures processes are environmentally safe.
- <u>Quality Assurance Specialist</u> - Makes sure all testing procedures are followed correctly and that the water meets all safety rules.

The Journey of Water Glossary

A <u>glossary</u> is like a mini-dictionary of terms with definitions.

Here's a glossary of terms associated with <u>Raw Water Treatment</u>.

<u>Aquifer</u> - Underground rock formations that hold groundwater, like a giant underground sponge that stores water between the spaces in rocks and soil.

<u>Bacteria</u> - Tiny living things that are so small you need a microscope to see them. Some bacteria in water can make people sick, which is why we need to clean water before drinking it.

<u>Chlorine</u> - A chemical that kills germs in water, similar to what's used in swimming pools to keep the water clean and safe.

<u>Clarification</u> - The process of removing all the hard, solid objects and particles from water to leave only clean, clear water. It happens in three stages: coagulation, flocculation, and sedimentation.

<u>Coagulation</u> - Adding special chemicals to water that make tiny pieces of dirt and waste stick together to form bigger chunks, kind of like how magnets stick together.

<u>Dam</u> - A wall built across a river to create a giant "water tank" that stores water for later use.

<u>Disinfection</u> - The step where chemicals like chlorine or special ultraviolet light are added to kill any remaining germs that could make us sick.

<u>Filtration</u> - Passing water through filters that work like giant sieves, letting clean water through while catching tiny bits of dirt that are still left behind.

<u>Flocculation</u> - Mixing water slowly with paddles (like a giant cake mixer) so the chunks formed during coagulation bump into each other and stick together to become even bigger and heavier.

<u>Flocs</u> - The larger, heavier chunks that form when dirt and waste particles stick together during coagulation and flocculation. They look like snowflakes!

Groundwater - Water found underground, beneath the Earth's surface, in the spaces between soil and rocks.

Pipes - Sturdy tubes that look like giant straws, made of materials like concrete, steel, or plastic, that carry water from place to place.

Pressure - The force that pushes water through pipes, kind of like when you squeeze a squirt gun to make water shoot out.

Pump Station - A building where pumps are installed to push water along through pipes, especially when water needs to travel uphill or to tall buildings.

Pumps - Machines that suck water up or push water along through pipes, working like powerful vacuum cleaners or fans.

Raw Water - Water that comes directly from rivers, lakes, dams, or underground that hasn't been cleaned yet and usually has dirt, bugs, leaves, and other things in it.

Reservoir - A giant container, either natural or man-made, that stores clean water until we need it at home, school, or work.

Screening - The first step in cleaning water, where large floating objects like leaves and twigs are removed by making water flow through or over large metal screens.

Sediment - The dirty particles that settle at the bottom of tanks during sedimentation, also called settlement.

Sedimentation - The process where water is left to stay very still so heavy flocs can slowly sink to the bottom of the tank, leaving cleaner water on top.

Strainer - A tool with tiny holes that separates things, like when Mom uses one to separate cooked spaghetti from water.

Surface Water - All the water you can see on Earth's surface, like rivers, streams, lakes, ponds, and oceans.

<u>Testing</u> - When engineers and scientists check water with special tools to search for any tiny germs that might still be hiding in the water.

<u>Ultraviolet Light</u> - Special light that kills germs in water, similar to how sunlight can kill some bacteria.

<u>Viruses</u> - Extremely tiny things that can make people sick and are even smaller than bacteria.

<u>Water Distribution System</u> - Also called a water supply system, this is the network of pipes, pumps, and storage tanks that transport clean water to our homes, schools, and workplaces.

<u>Water Intake Structures</u> - Special structures that work like giant straws, using pumps to suck water from rivers, lakes, or underground sources into pipes.

<u>Water Source</u> - The place where water comes from, which can be either surface water (like rivers and lakes) or groundwater (from underground).

<u>Water Storage Tanks</u> - Giant containers that store clean water until we need it. They can be tall water towers or big square or circular tanks, built above or below ground.

<u>Water Supply System</u> - Another name for the water distribution system that "supplies" or brings water to places where we need it.

<u>Water Tower</u> - A tall storage tank that holds clean water high above the ground, using gravity to help push water through pipes to homes and buildings.

<u>Water Treatment Plant</u> - Also called a Water Purification Plant, this is the special place where raw water goes through different cleaning processes to make it safe to drink.

The Journey of Water Quiz

1. What are the two main types of water sources?
   a) Clean water and dirty water
   b) Surface water and groundwater
   c) River water and lake water
   d) Hot water and cold water

2. What is raw water?
   a) Water that has been cleaned at a treatment plant
   b) Water that comes directly from the source and hasn't been cleaned yet
   c) Water that is too hot to drink
   d) Water that has been tested by scientists

3. What is the first step in the water treatment process?
   a) Disinfection
   b) Filtration
   c) Screening
   d) Testing

4. During coagulation, what happens to tiny pieces of dirt?
   a) They dissolve completely
   b) They stick together to form bigger chunks
   c) They sink to the bottom immediately
   d) They get filtered out

5. What do flocs look like?
   a) Raindrops
   b) Snowflakes
   c) Leaves
   d) Pebbles

6. Which engineer decides how big a water treatment plant needs to be?
   a) Mechanical Engineer
   b) Electrical Engineer
   c) Civil Engineer
   d) Chemical Engineer

7. What chemical is commonly used during disinfection?
   a) Salt
   b) Sugar
   c) Chlorine
   d) Soap

8. What do water intake structures work like?
   a) Giant straws
   b) Fishing nets
   c) Vacuum cleaners
   d) Garden hoses

9. Underground rock formations that hold groundwater are called:
   a) Reservoirs
   b) Aquifers
   c) Sediments
   d) Flocs

10. During sedimentation, heavy flocs:
    a) Float to the top
    b) Dissolve in the water
    c) Sink to the bottom
    d) Get mixed around

11. What professional studies tiny germs and bacteria in water?
   a) Civil Engineer
   b) Microbiologist
   c) Pump Station Operator
   d) Electrician

12. Water storage tanks can be built:
   a) Only above ground
   b) Only below ground
   c) Only in tall towers
   d) Above or below ground

13. What helps push water uphill through pipes?
   a) Gravity
   b) Wind
   c) Pump stations
   d) Water towers

14. Which step removes large floating objects like leaves and twigs?
   a) Screening
   b) Coagulation
   c) Flocculation
   d) Disinfection

15. What do filters act like during filtration?
   a) Giant magnets
   b) Giant sieves
   c) Giant fans
   d) Giant heaters

16. The dirty particles that settle during sedimentation are called:
    a) Flocs
    b) Bacteria
    c) Sediment
    d) Chlorine

17. Which engineer designs the chemical processes in water treatment?
    a) Civil Engineer
    b) Chemical Engineer
    c) Mechanical Engineer
    d) Systems Engineer

18. Water travels through pipes under:
    a) Vacuum
    b) Pressure
    c) Heat
    d) Cold

19. What kills remaining bacteria and viruses during disinfection?
    a) Heat and cold
    b) Pressure and vacuum
    c) Chemicals and ultraviolet light
    d) Screens and filters

20. Who runs the daily operations of cleaning water at treatment plants?
    a) Laboratory Analyst
    b) Water Treatment Plant Operator
    c) Environmental Scientist
    d) Pump Station Operator

21. During flocculation. water is mixed with:
    a) Spoons
    b) Paddles
    c) Brushes
    d) Fans

22. What professional maintains the special tools that measure water quality?
    a) Instrumentation Technician
    b) Millwright
    c) Pipefitter
    d) Control Room Operator

23. The network that transports clean water to homes is called a:
    a) Water treatment system
    b) Water distribution system
    c) Water collection system
    d) Water storage system

24. Which type of light can kill germs in water?
    a) Regular light bulbs
    b) Flashlight
    c) Ultraviolet light
    d) Candle light

25. What determines how big a water treatment plant needs to be?
    a) How much water needs cleaning and how dirty the water is
    b) Only how much water needs cleaning
    c) Only how dirty the water is
    d) The size of the city's population

26. Water found underground is called _____.

27. The place where water comes from is called a _____.

28. _____ are underground rock formations that hold groundwater.

29. Water that hasn't been cleaned yet is called _____.

30. The first step in water treatment that removes large objects is called _____.

31. During _____, special chemicals make dirt particles stick together.

32. The larger, heavier chunks formed during coagulation and flocculation are called _____.

33. During _____, water is left still so flocs can sink to the bottom.

34. _____ act like giant sieves to catch tiny bits of dirt.

35. _____ is a chemical commonly used to kill germs in water.

36. _____ light can also be used to kill bacteria and viruses.

37. A _____ is a wall built across a river to store water.

38. _____ work like giant straws to collect water from sources.

39. Clean water is stored in _____ and reservoirs.

40. Water travels through _____ to reach our homes.

41. _____ push water along pipes, especially uphill.

42. A _____ Engineer designs water treatment plants and distribution systems.

43. A _____ studies tiny germs and bacteria in water.

44. A _____ tests water samples to ensure they meet safety standards.

45. The _____ removes all solid objects and particles to leave clear water.

46. Water travels through pipes under _____.

47. The dirty particles that settle at the bottom are called _____.

48. A _____ Technician maintains equipment like screens and filters.

49. An _____ maintains special tools that measure water quality.

50. The force that pushes water through pipes is called _____.

True/False (Write T for True or F for False)

51. All living things need water to survive. _____

52. Surface water includes rivers, lakes, and oceans. _____

53. Groundwater can only be found in rivers. _____

54. Raw water is always safe to drink without treatment. _____

55. Screening is the last step in water treatment. _____

56. Coagulation makes tiny dirt particles stick together. _____

57. Flocs are heavier than water. _____

58. During sedimentation, flocs float to the top. _____

59. Filters work like giant sieves. _____

60. Chlorine is used to kill germs during disinfection. _____

61. Water treatment plants are all the same size. _____

62. Clean mountain lake water needs the same amount of treatment as muddy river water. _____

63. Civil Engineers determine how big water treatment plants need to be. _____

64. Water can be stored in both above-ground and below-ground tanks. _____

65. Pump stations help push water uphill. _____

66. Water travels through pipes without any pressure. _____

67. A Microbiologist studies tiny germs and bacteria in water. _____

68. Testing is done to make sure water is clean enough to drink. _____

69. Ultraviolet light can kill bacteria and viruses. _____

70. Water distribution systems only include pipes. _____

Quiz Answer Key

Multiple Choice	Fill-in-the-Blank	True/False
1. b	26. groundwater	51. T
2. b	27. water source	52. T
3. c	28. Aquifers	53. F
4. b	29. raw water	54. F
5. b	30. screening	55. F
6. c	31. coagulation	56. T
7. c	32. flocs	57. T
8. a	33. sedimentation	58. F
9. b	34. Filters	59. T
10. c	35. Chlorine	60. T
11. b	36. Ultraviolet	61. F
12. d	37. dam	62. F
13. c	38. Water intake structures	63. T
14. a	39. storage tanks	64. T
15. b	40. pipes	65. T
16. c	41. Pumps	66. F
17. b	42. Civil	67. T
18. b	43. Microbiologist	68. T
19. c	44. Water Quality Technician	69. T
20. b	45. clarification process	70. F
21. b	46. pressure	
22. a	47. sediment	
23. b	48. Maintenance	
24. c	49. Instrumentation Technician	
25. a	50. pressure	

Take a look at other subjects Lila and Andy are learning about...

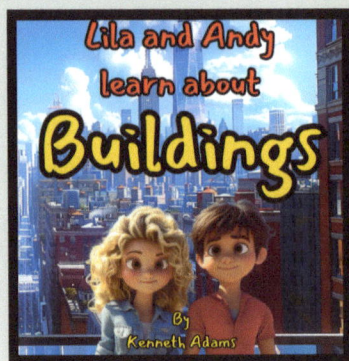
Lila and Andy learn about Buildings
By Kenneth Adams

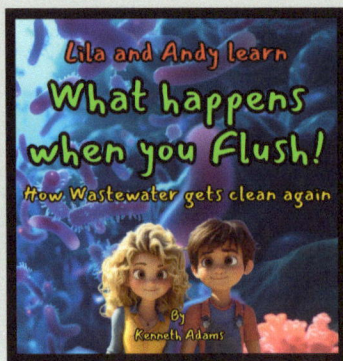
Lila and Andy learn What happens when you Flush!
How Wastewater gets clean again
By Kenneth Adams

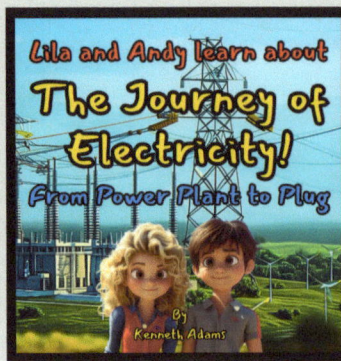
Lila and Andy learn about The Journey of Electricity!
From Power Plant to Plug
By Kenneth Adams

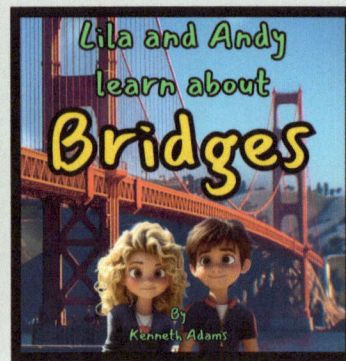
Lila and Andy learn about Bridges
By Kenneth Adams

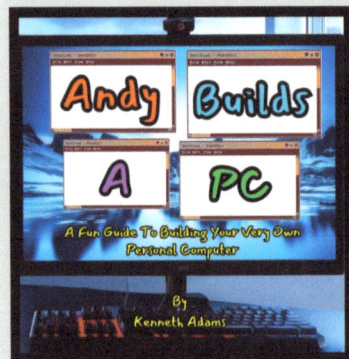
Andy Builds A PC
A Fun Guide To Building Your Very Own Personal Computer
By Kenneth Adams

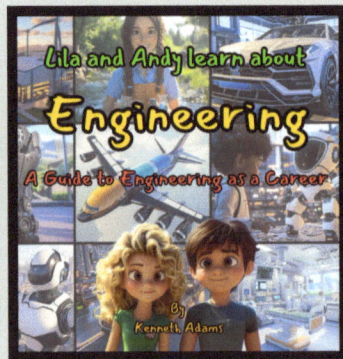
Lila and Andy learn about Engineering
A Guide to Engineering as a Career
By Kenneth Adams

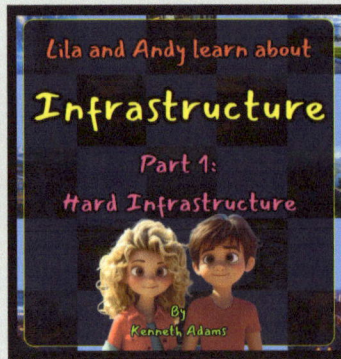
Lila and Andy learn about Infrastructure
Part 1:
Hard Infrastructure
By Kenneth Adams

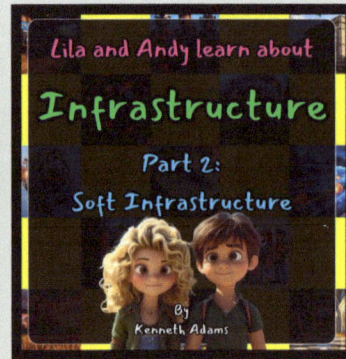
Lila and Andy learn about Infrastructure
Part 2:
Soft Infrastructure
By Kenneth Adams

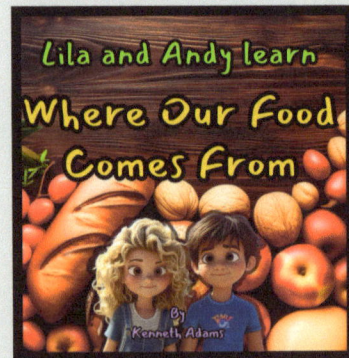
Lila and Andy learn Where Our Food Comes From
By Kenneth Adams

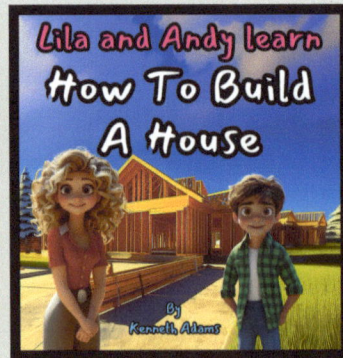
Lila and Andy learn How To Build A House
By Kenneth Adams

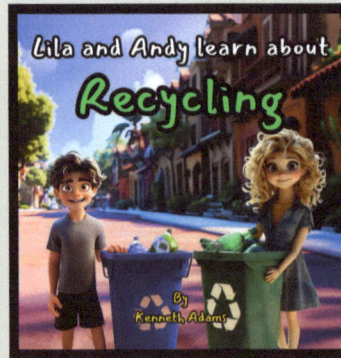
Lila and Andy learn about Recycling
By Kenneth Adams

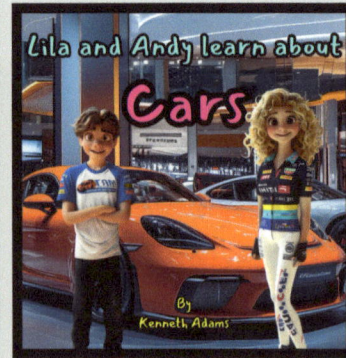
Lila and Andy learn about Cars
By Kenneth Adams

Lila and Andy learn about Safety on Ice
By Kenneth Adams

Lila and Andy learn about Winter Roads
By Kenneth Adams

Lila and Andy learn about Smart Cities
By Kenneth Adams

Lila and Andy learn about Digital Networks
How the Internet Connects Us
By Kenneth Adams

Lila and Andy learn about Biomimicry
ORGANIC
Kenneth Adams

Lila and Andy learn about Artificial Intelligence
Discover Large Language Models and Prompt Engineering
By Kenneth Adams

Lila and Andy learn about Climate Change
Understand Our Changing Planet
Kenneth Adams

Lila and Andy learn about Environmental Science
Protecting Earth Through Science
Kenneth Adams

Lila and Andy learn about The Carbon Cycle
Kenneth Adams

Lila and Andy learn about Data Science & Cryptography
Kenneth Adams

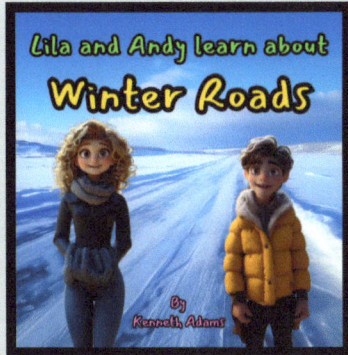

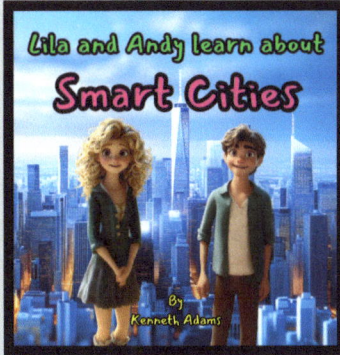

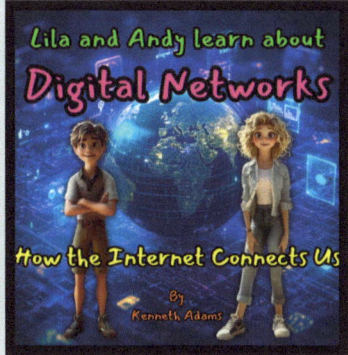

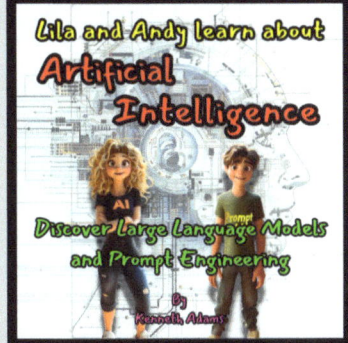

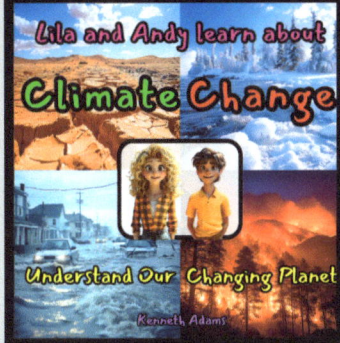

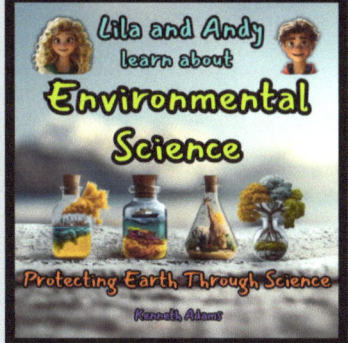

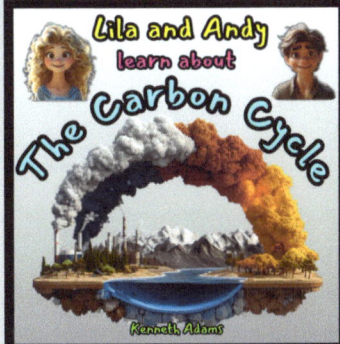

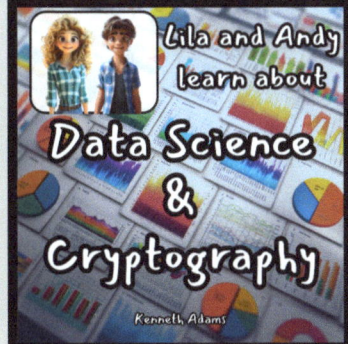

Available on Amazon.

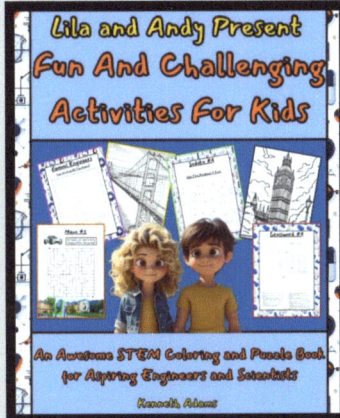

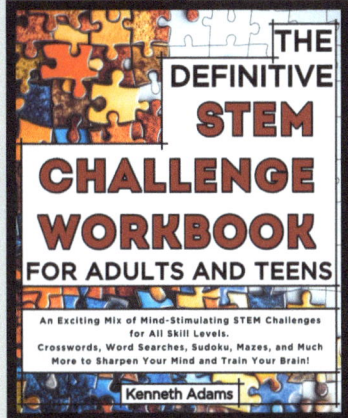

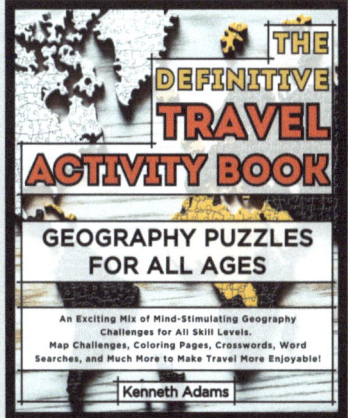

Lila and Andy Present Fun And Challenging Activities For Kids
An Awesome STEM Coloring and Puzzle Book for Aspiring Engineers and Scientists
Kenneth Adams

THE DEFINITIVE STEM CHALLENGE WORKBOOK FOR ADULTS AND TEENS
An Exciting Mix of Mind-Stimulating STEM Challenges for All Skill Levels.
Crosswords, Word Searches, Sudoku, Mazes, and Much More to Sharpen Your Mind and Train Your Brain!
Kenneth Adams

THE DEFINITIVE TRAVEL ACTIVITY BOOK
GEOGRAPHY PUZZLES FOR ALL AGES
An Exciting Mix of Mind-Stimulating Geography Challenges for All Skill Levels.
Map Challenges, Coloring Pages, Crosswords, Word Searches, and Much More to Make Travel More Enjoyable!
Kenneth Adams